The Great Story of Gretna

Romance, Remembrance, History, Legacy.

Heath Hampson

Four books on Gretna are displayed in Ewart's Library, the main library for Dumfries and Galloway.

Gretna Green and the Nether Border by Shaw

Gretna Green Memoirs by Robert Elliott

Gretna Green and it's Traditions by Claverhouse Published 1905

Old Gretna by Rhona Wilson

This book is for children and adults.

Please keep it safe for future generations to read.

I have always been interested in British History, I like to know what was going on before we were born and what life was like in days gone by.

I have always wanted to create a book on Gretna. It's a wonderful town with an amazing history.

I don't go into detail on some of the topics, just lots of pictures with a couple of lines or paragraph.

I would like you to delve deeper by visiting Ewart's Library, Devils Porridge Museum etc, and do your own research into this fascinating area.

Hopefully in a few decades time someone else will add to the books written on our area to add to **The Great Story of Gretna**.

Heath Hampson

January 2020

I0166803

The Border Reivers 1296 ~ 1603.

The names on the map above are of the families or clans. Armstrong, Graham, Johnstone, Maxwell and many more...

Border Reivers were raiders along the England-Scotland border from the late 13th century to the beginning of the 17th century.

It was during these turbulent years that raids took place on moonlit autumn nights, against anyone who was not of that family or clan.

Cattle, sheep and horses were the main prizes, but literally anything of value and could be carried, would be brought back. This also included people for ransom.

Gilnockie/Hollows Tower.

On the banks of the River Esk. It was home to one of the most famous Border Reivers, Johnnie Armstrong of Gilnockie.

Border Reivers Statue at Reivers Court, Carlisle.

View from Sark Bridge. The River Sark has been the border between England and Scotland since 1603.

The mouth of the River Sark, 300 yards from the Sark Bridge.

Down the Solway. Many Battles were fought in the area for the control of the border. The most famous was the Battle of Sark on 23rd October 1448.

The Earl of Northumberland led a troop of 6,000 Englishmen into Scotland where they made camp near The Lochmaben Stone. A large battle with 4,000 Scots ended with a Scottish victory, with over 3,000 English soldiers killed. The Scots lost 600 men.

The Lochmaben Stone.

The stone dates back to 3,000 B.C.

Lochmaben Stone stands in a field 500 yards from the mouth of the River Sark.

7 feet high and 18 feet in girth.

.

Robert Burns 1759 ~ 1796

The national poet of Scotland. Famous for the poem sang at New Year's Eve, Auld Lang Syne. He was one time employed as a Revenues Officer in the Dumfries area. In March 1792, at the mouth of the River Sark, he was involved in the dramatic seizure of a large smuggling vessel called The Rosamond. He was assisted by a strong party of the 3rd Regiment of Scots Dragoons.

Robert Burns Statue, Dumfries

Quintinshill Rail Disaster Saturday 22nd May 1915 at 6.50am

A troop train carrying 500 soldiers of the 7th Royal Scots Territorial Battalion travelled south on their way to fight in Gallipoli during World War One.

Another train travelling north on the same line collided with the oncoming train which burst into flames.

While survivors staggered from the wreckage, the Carlisle Express also ran into it causing more destruction.

Once the fire was extinguished, 82 bodies were unrecognisable and 50 were not traced at all.

Two signalmen, James Tinsley and George Meakin made several careless mistakes which resulted in Britain's worst rail disaster.

Most of the troops had come from Leith and Musselburgh, their funerals were held in Rosebank Cemetery two days later.

In total 230 people died and 246 were injured.

On the troop train, only 58 men and 7 officers escaped Quintinshill alive and uninjured.

They should have carried on their journey to fight in Gallipoli but were declared unfit and sent back home to Leith and Musselburgh.

His Majesty's Factory Gretna
&
The Gretna Girls

British Soldiers in the trenches in need of ammunition

In 1915, Britain was losing the war due to the lack of ammunition.

Building HM Factory Gretna

Gretna owes its existence to the government's decision during World War One to build an ammunitions factory near the Solway Firth.

The Government named it, His Majesty's Factory Gretna.

Wooden Huts & Hostels

The quiet surrounding area, previously populated by isolated farms, suddenly needed to provide accommodation.

First for the large number of construction workers, many from Ireland, Dumfries & Galloway and Cumbria.

Then the 30,000 munitions workers and their families.

Central Offices on Glasgow Road.

Formerly a large timber building where administration for the whole factory was carried out.

Central Offices Now the North Car Park for Gretna Gateway.

Surrone House Farm Now the Surrone House Guest House

Surrone Farm was one of a handful of buildings built before the township of Gretna in 1916. It became the pasteurising plant, ensuring a safe, longer lasting milk for the new Gretna township. There were two deliveries each day.

Another farm close by was **The Beeches** at the corner of Loanwath Road and Sarkfoot Road.

George & Hannah Hardisty My great grand parents moved to Gretna in 1915 from Thirlmere in Cumbria. George helped build the ammunition factory and the town of Gretna. They lived in one of the wooden huts, they had five sons and three daughters.

They were married in 1905. This is George and Hannah at their 50th wedding anniversary in 1955. The lady bottom left wearing the white blouse is my nana, Mary Nelson.

The Gretna Girls

The workforce, mostly female were drawn from all over Britain.

They would be working in the biggest ammunition factory in the world! HM Factory Gretna.

Scientists & Specialists

They were joined by chemists, physicians, engineers and various specialists from all over the world.

The Gretna Girls made up 60 percent of the factories workforce and were aged between 16 and 21 years of age.

The workers were employed to manufacture RDB Cordite, a new form of munitions propellent.

The Devils Porridge

The workers produced Cordite, a mixture of guncotton and nitro-glycerine. It was a volatile mix which had a resemblance to porridge. Devils Porridge!

HM Factory Gretna made more RDB Cordite than all the other munitions factories combined.

Providing the much-needed ammunition for our soldiers fighting on the front line.

Timbertown

The workers and their families started life in Gretna in temporary wooden huts and hostels which earned the name, Timbertown.

Empire Way & Dominion Road

The junction from Empire Way to Dominion Road. The Hospital (Now the Masonic Lodge) the white building can be seen in the distance.

Raydale Park, the home of Gretna Football Club and the Gretna Social Club were built where the hostels once stood in the top right corner of the picture.

Gretna 1916 ~ Central Avenue

The Government realised the importance of the factory to the war effort so decided to establish a permanent town.

Gretna had all the facilities imaginable to keep the workforce happy in their vital work.

The shops consisted of a café, co-op grocery, furnishers, bakers, drapers and boots, also a dairy.

Cinema on Central Avenue

The Cinema opened on 23rd September 2016 with seating for 700 people.

Gretna locals in 1917 walking up and down Central Avenue.

The Cinema is on the left.

Gretna School

Gretna School opened in 1916 with 215 pupils on roll. Notice the train track running down the road and the little boy next to the gate.

Train outside St Andrews Church of Scotland, Central Avenue.

Central Kitchens, Steam Laundry, Bakery, Garages and Workshops

On the south side of Gretna, close to the Empire Way and Dominion Road Junction. This collection of buildings kept Gretna running smoothly.

The kitchens supplied 14,000 meals per day.

The steam laundry washed and cleaned 50,000 items per week.

King George V and Queen Mary visit Gretna

In May 1917 King George V and Queen Mary visited Gretna in recognition of the workers remarkable achievements.

Look at the lovely smiles from The Gretna Girls as King George V walks along Central Avenue.

Women's Police Force, King George V and Queen Mary

Gretna was home to one of the first women's police forces. They looked after the moral welfare of the female workers and kept the factory rules.

Gretna's Women's Police Force

The Staff Club Now the Hunters Lodge Hotel

The Staff Club, with seating for 200. The King and Queen dined here in May 1917 enjoying a roast beef dinner.

The Doctor's House Now the Gables Hotel

The residence of Senior Medical Officer Dr Carlyle.

The Fire Station now retail outlets on Annan Road

H. M. Factory Gretna Fire Engine

152 fires were attended to from 1916 to 1918.

Anti-Aircraft Building across from the main HM Factory Offices, Glasgow Road, now the north car park of the shopping centre.

Telephone Exchange across from the main HM Factory Offices, Glasgow Road, now the north car park of the shopping centre.

The Labour Exchange ~ Now the Gretna Inn / Crossways Inn

This building is where the 30,000 workers collected their wages.

The Union Jack Hotel Now the Solway Lodge

The Institute Now the Richard Greenhow Centre

Hall, club and recreational rooms for male and female operatives.

Richard Greenhow was a popular local councillor.

The Institute with train track running past.

Wooden path where King George V and Queen Mary walked across in May 1917.

The Border Hall (Dance Hall) Central Avenue, where the doctor's surgery is now situated.

The Border Hall

The Border Hall (Dance Hall) was completed in 39 days.

The pine floor was laid down in one night.

The Dance Hall could accommodate 800 people.

The Hospital, Annan Road, Now the Masonic Lodge.

Police Barracks, Annan Road, now residential accommodation.

Gretna Post Office Now the Chemists, Annan Road

Over four million letters were handled, 87,000 postal orders were sold and 51,000 telegrams delivered.

All Saints Episcopal Church Opposite the chemist, opened in September 1917.

St Ninians Roman Catholic Church Opened in April 1918

Sold to Heath & Jackie Hampson in 2003 and renamed Anvil Hall.

St Andrew's Church ~ Junction of Central Avenue and Loanwath Road, Opened in March 1918

World War One
1914 – 1918

Thank you to the men who helped build
HM Factory Gretna

Thank you to

The Gretna Girls

who helped our soldiers win our freedom

We Will Remember Them

GRAITNEY
(Gretna)

1693 ~ 1916

The Village Green,
Springfield,
Weddings &
The Gretna 'Priests'

Graitney Hall (Gretna Hall) and the Village Green, Graitney Estate belonged to the Johnstone family. In 1693, the parliament of Scotland passed an act which allowed William Johnstone of Graitney permission to have a weekly market on the village green. There were cottages at the bottom of Graitney Hall, they are no longer standing. One was used by 'Gretna Priest' Joseph Paisley.

The village green at Graitney. This is where the name Gretna Green came from, Graitney Green.

GRETNA CHURCH.

Graitney Parish Church

The name Graitney was used in church records until 1st February 1916 and thereafter the name Gretna is used.

Prince Charlie's Cottage next to the Parish Church is one of the oldest buildings in the area.

Bonnie Prince Charlie's army passed through Gretna on their retreat from England in 1745. Prince Charlie spent a night in the cottage.

Graitney Hall ~ Now Gretna Hall Hotel In 1700, Colonel James Johnstone built Graitney Hall as a family mansion for his bride Isabella. Sixty years later it became the property of the Earl of Hopetoun. It was under his ownership it was converted for use as an inn around 1793. Weekly markets on the village green were very popular, as well as couples eloping from England to be married.

Gretna Hall passed into the hands of other families, Maxwells and Maitlands, finally the estate, a very extensive one, was divided into several farms and sold.

Jim Jackson worked at Gretna Hall for many years. He knew the true history of the area. Weddings, Springfield and the 'Gretna Priests'.

Graitney Loaning

Travelling the two minute walk up Graitney Loaning up to Headless Cross stood cottages at Sarkside. Henry's shop is located in the middle of the row.

Headless Cross 1900 At the top of Graitney Loaning was five old coaching roads which formed the junction called Headless Cross. Top right in the picture above the small building is the top of the Free Church built in 1896.

The building on the left was converted into a museum in 1904 by Hugh Mackie. The two gentlemen in the picture will have been Peter Dickson who was a joiner by trade, and John Dickson who was a shoemaker.

Free Church at Headless Cross built in 1894

The stone at the side of the church:

This Stone Was Laid by Thomas McKie. Esq 26th September 1894

Springfield Turning right at Headless Cross was the village of Springfield which was closer to England than Graitney. Springfield's position just over the border gave it an edge over its rivals in the marriage business.

The Maxwell Arms Inn the large building on the right was one of the buildings used as a place for couples to get married. It was named after Sir William Maxwell who completed building the village in 1791.

The Queens Head Hotel Further down the village and even closer to the border, giving it a better position to attract the eloping couples. Built in 1760.

The Blacksmith's Myth and the 'Gretna Priests' from 1730 to 2019

The men who performed the marriages were from a variety of backgrounds.

You will notice from the list below that there is no Blacksmith. A Blacksmith never married anyone. Blacksmiths were not in the area during the time couples came over the border after 1754. The Marriage Act of 1754 in England stated couples had to be 21 years of age and have their parent's consent to be married. In Scotland you could marry aged 16.

The 'Priests' from 1730 to 1908

1. Colthard, schoolmaster
2. Scott, mill wright
3. Gordon, soldier
4. Paisley, fisherman and tobacconist
5. Johnstone, ferryman
6. Brown, shoemaker
7. Lang, David, pedlar
8. Elliot, Robert, post-boy
9. Elliot, Andrew, farm hand
10. Linton, butler
11. Linton, assistant, and son of above
12. Little, beer shop keeper
13. Lang, Simon, weaver
14. McQueen, toll-keeper
15. Jardine, decoy stonebreaker
16. Graham, poacher
17. Ferguson, inn keeper
18. Beatie, toll-keeper
19. Beattie, daughter of above who disguised in male attire acted as his assistant
20. Gibson, protégé of Linton and railway guard
21. Douglas, local dandie
22. Murray, stonemason
23. Blythe, fisherman
24. Lang, William, weaver and assistant to his father Simon

These were the people who married the couples up to 1856 when the marriage act changed again. A new marriage act, Lord Broughams Marriage Act in 1855 stated that the bride or groom had to live in Scotland for 21 days before they could marry their partner.

25. Peter Dickson, Joiner, married couples after the 1856 marriage act until the late 1800's and to his death in 1907
26. William McCartney, Shoemaker, married couples in the Queens Head from 1907.

Joseph Paisley There were weddings before the Marriage Act of 1754, these were performed by a Mr Colthard who was a schoolmaster, Mr Scott who was a millwright and Major Gordon from Rigg, an old soldier in the British Grenadiers. He wore his full uniform when performing the wedding ceremonies. Major Gordons nephew was Joseph Paisley. He was a fisherman and a tobacconist. Fisherman in those days meant smuggler. Paisley was born near Annan in 1733, he lived in one of the cottages across from the village green before he moved to Springfield in 1791 where he lived across from the Queens Head Hotel. He married many couples in his first house near the village green and in the Queens Head Hotel and became the first great 'Gretna Priest'.

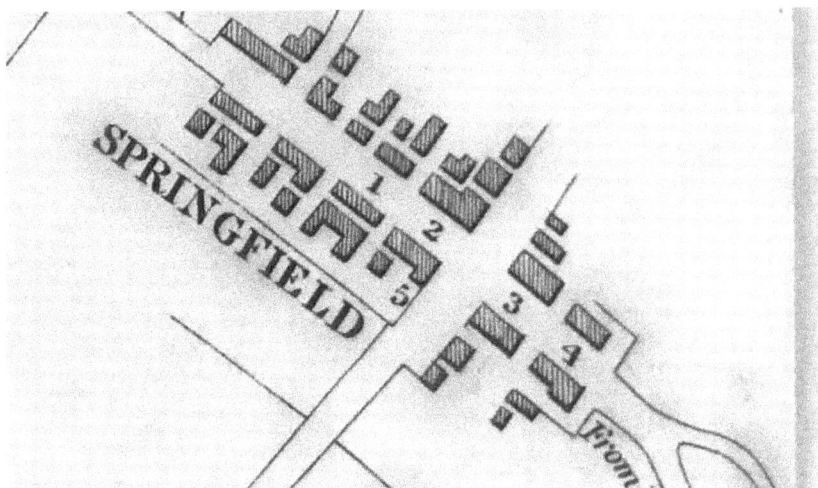

House Number 5 across from the Queens Head is where Paisley lived and died.

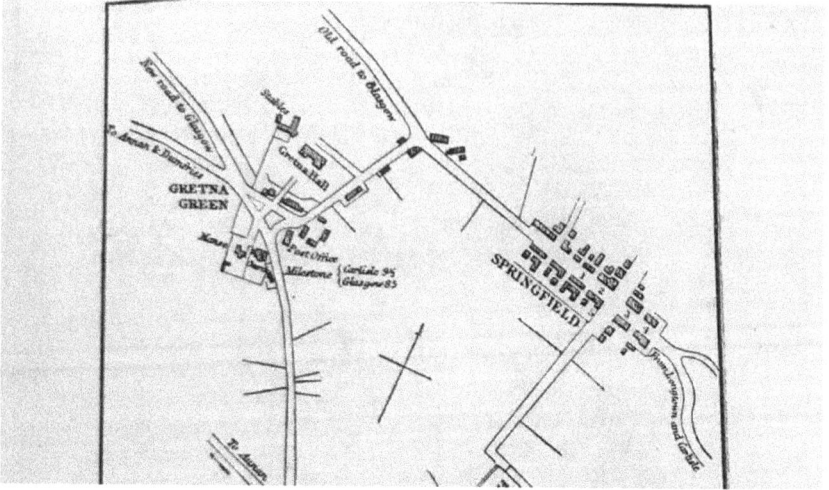

The houses and Inns in Springfield where some of 'Priests' lived, died, and where many of the couples married. In the map below, house number 1. is where David Lang died. 2. Queens Head Hotel. 3. Simon Lang lived, 4. David Land lived and performed weddings. 5. Where the most famous 'Priest' Joseph Paisley died.

Joseph Paisley died 9th January 1811 aged 79. He is laid to rest in Gretna Parish Church Graveyard.

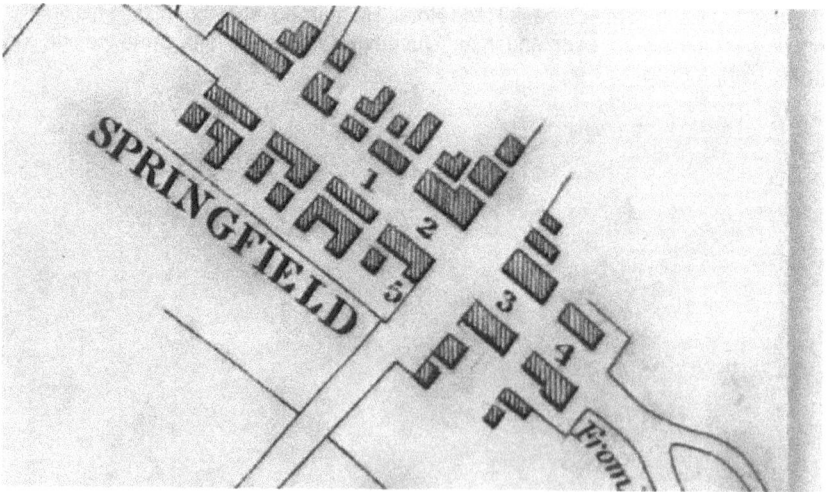

David Lang was born in 1755 and died in 1827. In his early youth he went to Lancashire as a draper and pedlar. He was kidnapped by the pressgang and forced to serve in the navy for a few years. The ship in which he sailed was captured by Paul Jones, the famous pirate, but Lang managed to escape and return to his native place where entered the 'Marriage Trade' in 1792.

Robert Elliot married Joesph Paisley's granddaughter Ann Graham in January 1811. Paisley died shortly after the marriage. From the year 1810 Robert Elliot lived in the Queens Head Hotel where Paisley performed the marriages. Soon after Joseph Paisley died, Robert became a 'Gretna Priest'. Robert died in 1840.

John Linton was perhaps the only 'Gretna Priest' with any real respectability.

He was the ex-butler of Sir James Graham of Netherby, Cumbria.

John Linton took a lease of Graitney Hall (Gretna Hall) in 1825.

He was of fine appearance and a popular member of the community. He was friendly with Mr Morgan, the Minister at Graitney Parish Church.

Mr Morgan advised Linton to do away with the services of the Springfield priests who could not be relied on, and often came the worse for too much alcohol.

Graitney Hall favoured by the rich and famous, and Linton, a refined and dignified man, knew exactly how to treat his aristocratic guests.

Captains, Generals, and gentlemen of all sorts married at Graitney Hall.

On 7th May 1846, an Italian prince came to Graitney Hall, Carlo Ferdinando, brother of the King of Naples, followed in 1847 by an Italian Duke.

Linton kept a record of all the marriages he performed, he was meticulous about what entries were made.

John Linton married more than a thousand couples at Graitney Hall before his death in 1851.

Thomas Little He was nicknamed 'Tom the Piper' for his skills on the bagpipes.

Tom moved to Springfield and took out a public-house licence.

The sign above the door wrote 'The Gretna Wedding Inn'. He had to remove the sign as there was a house across the road already called 'The Wedding Inn'.

Thomas Little needed a name for his sign. In his early life he was apprentice to a Blacksmith, this is where the blacksmith's myth was born.

He called his Inn 'the Blacksmith's Shop' The weddings were performed over an anvil and at the end of the ceremony he would say 'I hear by forge two lives together' and then strike the anvil.

T' BLACKSMITH'S SHOP INN.
The figure in the doorway is the late priest—Peter Dickson.

An old picture of where Thomas Little had his Inn and Priest Peter Dickson, picture below who performed weddings in the late 1800's, Peter Dickson died in 1907.

Simon Lang Son of David Lang was nicknamed 'Simmie' or 'Sim.' He was a weaver in Springfield but also a 'Priest' from 1827 to 1872.

William Lang, Simon's son received the decreasing 'mantle of glory' by becoming a 'priest' in 1872 after his father's death. He is remembered by most in the area in his official position as postman, which he filled until about eighteen months before his death in 1896.

Thomas Johnstone, Gretna Priest 1909.

David Ramsey MacIntosh. Priest at Gretna Hall from 1938. During his career he was rivalled by Richard Rennison, who performed wedding ceremonies at the museum at Headless Cross, Rennison from Shannock in Northumberland performed ceremonies from 1926 to 1940.

Simon Beattie 1830 a new bridge was built over the River Sark with it a toll road into Scotland. A toll house was built and named Allison's Bank Toll Bar with Simon Beattie as toll keeper. He started performing weddings and became very successful.

Allison's Bank Toll Bar and the Sark Bridge. Simon Beattie was 'Priest' from 1836 to 1843. On one weekend between 4am on Saturday morning and Sunday evening Simon married no less than 45 couples.

He made enough money during his time as a 'Priest' that he went on to buy a farm on the Mossknow estate, He is the only 'priest' to leave 'the trade.'

Sark Bank Hotel Now the Gretna Chase Hotel. John Murray was a stonemason but continued the trade as 'priest' at the toll bar from 1843 to 1856. The fame of the toll bar was at its height, on one night alone John married sixty-one couples. He built a comfortable house on the English side of the River Sark intending it for a hotel. Lord Brougham's Marriage Act came into force just as the building was completed which meant a big decline in weddings in the area.

The River Sark is the border between England and Scotland. The Gretna Chase Hotel is in England with a Scottish Post Code and Phone Number. John Hall owned 'the Chase' in the 70's and early 80's, then the Monaghan family, Jim. Pat, Claire & Siobhan into 21st Century.

1908 William Irving McCartney – Shoemaker the Marriage Act of 1856 saw a big decline in wedding ceremonies but couples still came to marry in the area. Two 'Priests' into the 1900's were Peter Dickson, a joiner and William McCartney who was a local shoemaker in Springfield. He performed wedding ceremonies in the Queens Head Hotel.

Terms Moderate to Fishing and other parties.

JAMES MOSCROP, Proprietor.

O, Yes! YOU can still be Married at Gretna Green.

If Scotch—at a moment's notice. If English, or Foreign, 21 days' residence is required of one of the contracting parties.

Apply to

W. Irving Mc.Cartney,

Shoemaker, SPRINGFIELD, GRETNA. Carlisle,

who still marries in "Lord Erskine's room."

Williams advertisement in a local publication in 1908.

Williams neighbour in Springfield was the local blacksmith with his own Smithy, his name was William Davidson, and no, he didn't perform wedding ceremonies.

Museum at Headless Cross and the Blacksmiths Myth.

Since Lord Hardwicks Marriage Act of 1754 there were various places in the area where the marriages took place.

The houses of the 'Priests' Joseph Paisley, the Lang's, the Elliot's and Tom the Piper, etc. Graitney Hall, The Maxwell Arms Inn, Queens Head Hotel, Allison's Bank Toll and of course Gretna Parish Church where many locals have had their wedding ceremony.

In 1907 a petition was prepared and extensively signed by residents in the area for the attention of Mr Gordon, Chief Constable of Dumfriesshire. It was to stop the museum false advertising and propagating the Blacksmith's myth. The Dumfries Standard wrote in the **30th October 1907** edition the following:

Gretna Green Marriages

Another Wedding – Propagating a Myth – Appeal to the Chief Constable

The romantic traditions of Gretna Green and the contiguous village of Springfield were revived in a small way on Friday afternoon last, when another of the irregular marriages which have taken place there at intervals for time immemorial was performed. But that incident, all important though it was to the contracting parties, has been dwarfed by an agitation which has been set on foot to seek the intervention of Mr. Gordon, Chief Constable of Dumfriesshire, in a matter connected to the marriages there.

It might have been expected that weddings 'a la young Lochinvar' which have made Gretna Green famous for all time, would have ceased on the alteration of the Scotch law requiring that the parties must have lived twenty-one consecutive days in Scotland, but marriages by declaration have nevertheless continued to take place in the vicinity of Gretna Green.

Records show that during successive generations persons of the name of Paisley, Elliot, Linton, Douglas, Little, Murray, and Lang have in their turn assisted at the tying of 'the knot.' Three generations of the Langs played the role of 'priest,' a title in which they received in respect of their services, and the last of that ilk in the district, Willie Lang, the village postman, died in 1896.

But the district was never without it's 'priest,' and Lang, who resided in Springfield, was succeeded by Peter Dickson, who, who we have it on authority, 'tied the nuptial knot as firm as in the palmiest days,' Dickson, who was a joiner to trade, died in September last in Carlisle Infirmary. The house where he lived, and in which he had often performed the marriage ceremony, was the property of Mr. Hugh Mackie, Gretna House.

With the view of attracting visitors to the place, a portion of the house has been laid off as a 'museum,' in which are exhibited relics of Willie Lang, pictures of his predecessors, and some articles of greater or lesser antiquarian interest. Over the front of 'the museum,' situated at Headless Cross, within two minutes' walk of Gretna Green, are the words in large letters, "Old Priest's." Steps were also taken to advertise the museum and encourage a continuance of the irregular marriages by distribution of circulars to motorists and others, and which have also found their way into the public-houses of the surrounding district.

The circular sets forth the interesting character of Gretna Green from its romantic associations, and states that "there has been established at the village a pleasant old curiosity shop in the old smithy buildings where the runaway marriage business was and is carried on." It is also stated that a proprietor in the district offers any lady who comes to Gretna to be made a bride the gift of half-a-guinea or its equivalent, while the driver of the happy pair has 'just to name what he would like to refresh the inner man and it will be supplied gratis."

The issue of this circular broadcast has been followed by the preparation of a petition, which has already extensively signed. It is addressed to Mr Gordon, chief constable of Dumfriesshire, and is in the name of residents, heritors, and other interested in Gretna parish and the public welfare.

It calls attention to 'the trade pursued in the shop situated at Headless Cross, in the parish of Gretna,' and protests 'against the circular which is being freely distributed and tends to sustain a widely-believed myth that Gretna Green marriages were performed in the blacksmith's shop, the face being that there was no blacksmith's shop in Gretna Green at that time.' The prayer of the petition is that Mr. Gordon will interest himself in the matter sufficiently to enquire into it, and if he should find good and sufficient cause to use his authority to stop the misrepresentations which are being so widely disseminated.

The museum is now under the charge of Mrs. Graham, and she is also 'priestess.' When on Friday afternoon a couple of young people presented themselves desiring to be united, she obligingly placed her services at their disposal, and the fact that she had herself been married by the late Peter Dickson in the same irregular way might have carried assurance, but the man hinted that he did 'not care about being married by a woman,' and the services of John Dickson, shoemaker, who assisted on some occasions, were requisitioned, and the ceremony completed.

The entry in the register was in the following terms: 'Hugh Corley, from the parish of Annan, and Alice Campbell, from the parish of Annan, being now both here present, and having declared to me that they are single persons, have now been married after the manner of the laws of Scotland. As Witness our hands at Gretna, 25th October, 1907. – Hugh Corley, Alice Campbell; witnesses, James Davidson, Janet Graham."

While having entered their names as having come from the parish of Annan, it is understood the contracting parties belong to Glasgow.

From the Dumfries Standard in the **30th October 1907** edition.

Gretna Green Marriages

Another Wedding – Propagating a Myth – Appeal to the Chief Constable

Registrars from 1855 to 1993
William Duff 1855 to 1876
Francis Kerr 1877 to 1893
J H Lamont 1894 to 1909
A Kirkpatrick 1910 to 1929
J W Bryson 1930 to 1958
Robert Hastings 1959 to 1971 Assistant Pat Bryden
Pat Bryden 1971 to 1990

Registration Office, Glasgow Road, 1962 It was situated where the outlet village north car park is now, far righthand corner. Picture Below: Sign at the driveway entrance to the Registration Office, 1962.

Gretna Registration Office Glasgow Road 1962

Gretna Registration Office 1986

Here you could be married, pay your council rent or have a tooth out. A dentist also used the small building.

Pat Bryden outside the Registration Office in 1986. Pat married over 10,000 couples during her time as Gretna Registrar. She received an MBE in 1990.

The couple Pat Bryden married stayed in the Romeo & Juliet Honeymoon Suite at the Gretna Chase Hotel.

The Callander Hamilton Bridge spanned the Sark River. The fields in the background is now the shopping centre.

New Gretna Registration Office opened on 2nd September 1991 by Pat Bryden MBE. It was extended in 1997.

Solway Suite at Gretna Registration Office.

Alison Quigley, Jane Chandler, Pamela Dodd, Kathryn Graham & Gwen Bruce are some of the registrars from 1991 to 2020.

Alister Lynn Photography & Gretna Wedding Bureau Alister started his photography business in Annan in 1968. The Registration Office created a wedding brochure in which Alister would advertise in the first six pages. He and his wife Rhona started Gretna Wedding Bureau and with the help of son Mark they have been the leaders in the Gretna wedding industry for many years.

Mike and Valerie Phillips. Gretna Hall 1973 to 2006

Mike started at Gretna Hall in 1973, Val in 1974, they married in 1975. They ran Gretna Hall for many years, weddings, coach tours and did a lot for the local community.

Anvil Hall, former Saint Ninians Roman Catholic Church.

Jackie and Heath Hampson bought Saint Ninians in 2003 and renamed it Anvil Hall.

We started our online wedding business from our council house in Gretna in 1998, before the likes of Google, Facebook, YouTube etc. We were the first Gretna wedding business to go online and over the years we have helped over 10,000 couples with their wedding plans.

We helped a lot of local businesses get online too, and we also helped a few people start their own wedding businesses.

1917 – 2017 Centenary Garden at Anvil Hall

Nine couples have their names set in stone in the centenary garden with a family tree. There is also a time capsule secretly hidden in the ground at Anvil Hall.

The nine couples who are forever part of the Anvil Hall Legacy.

Kirsty & Mike Linnett
5th November 2015 ~ Wigan

Julie & Gary Corbett
4th May 2017 ~ Grangemouth

Joanne & John Hirst
28th June 2014 ~ Mexborough

Rob & Denise Dunn
20th August 2016 ~ Redcar

Patricia & Paul Tyson
22nd August 2016 ~ Berkhamsted

Samantha & Trevor Durrant
18th July 2015 ~ Roughton, Norwich

Mark & Helen Willis
31st December 2004 ~ Clitheroe

Julie & Craig Elliott
16th May 2015 ~ Barnoldswick, Lancs

Michelle & Tomasz Osadinska
8th September 2017 ~ Hatfield, Herts

Some of the Gretna Priests from the 1990's to the present day.

Laurie Dennison, David Bennett, Adam Barr, David Crouchley, Ian Meredith, Bob Taylor, Bob Briscoe, John Carr, David Batson, Brian Ridley, Bob White, Ella Pennington,

Jack Strachan

Donald Frith

Sandy Jamieson

Mark Smith

1754

2020

And the Future

The Ministers & Registrars
continue to perform the
wedding ceremonies

Just like the
Gretna 'Priests'

Gretna
Football Club

Built by the people of Gretna

For the people of Gretna

The driving force behind the formation of Gretna FC was Jock Kerr. Here he is front row on the right. The picture is Jock in his team photograph for Brentford FC in London.

Jocks two sons, Billy, back row on the left, and Tommy front row second left, had just returned from serving in World War Two. The black shorts they wore were made from the blackout blinds for the house windows. They started off playing their games at Station Park on Mackie's field. Their first season was in the Dumfries Junior League.

They joined the Carlisle District League in their second season.

Some local people of Gretna gave £10 each to the football club funds, £10 was a weekly wage in 1946.

The young lad at the front is George White, his son David and grandson Nikki would go on to play for Gretna.

Success in the 1950's in the Carlisle District League was helped by the building of a club house in 1957.

The success continued into the 1960's and in 1970 a new social club was built and the membership swelled to 1,500 members.

Continued success in the 1970's with six consecutive Carlisle District League titles proved the club was becoming too strong.

More trophies were being lifted in the Carlisle District League until season 1981/82 Gretna Football Club joined the Northern League.

Gordon Park, back row third from the left was the team manager and in the first season they finished runner up and promoted to the first division.

The clubs next manager was Mick McCartney. Gretna FC spent nine successful seasons in the Northern League with back to back championships from 1990/91 and 1991/92.

Gretna's successful Sunday Market helped build a stronger team and Raydale Park Stadium.

In season 1992/93, Gretna moved to a higher level of football, the HFS Loans League.

There have been some big games played at Raydale Park. In 1988, Gretna played the first team of Glasgow Rangers to raise money for the victims of the nearby Lockerbie Air Disaster. Gretna won the match 2-1.

Gretna FC reached the first round of the FA Cup on Saturday 16th November 1991 against Rochdale FC.

The BBC Match of the Day programme showed the game on the evening.

The game ended 1-1, Rochdale won the replay.

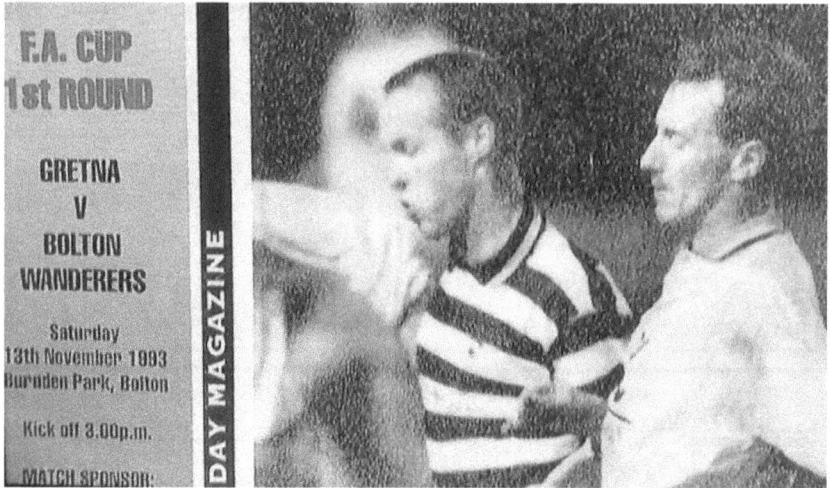

Two years later, on Saturday 13th November 1993 Gretna FC again reached the first round of the FA Cup, this time against Bolton Wanderers. Gretna were winning 2-0 but the final score was 3-2 to Bolton.

Gretna Football Club entered the Scottish Football League in 2002 and with the financial backing of Brooks Mileson, Gretna Football Club 'Lived the Dream'

Sky Sports TV presenter Jeff Stelling announced that Gretna had scored a winning goal in the 90th minute against Ross County FC to send Gretna Football Club into the Scottish Premier League.

Gretna Football Club reached the Scottish Cup Final in 2006 against Hearts.

Team Manager Rowan Alexander lead the team out for this very special occasion.

Players from the original team started in 1946, Davie Scott, Goalkeeper Eric Mitchell and Tommy Kerr. It looks like Davie is saying to Tommy 'Do you wish you had your football boots on Tommy?'. The Scottish Cup visited Gretna the week before the cup final.

Johnny Kerr, Tommy Kerr's son on the left, Keith Rhodes, right in the picture. Keith was Gretna Football Club secretary for many years and played a big part in Gretna FC's successes over the years. We all had a good time at the Scottish Cup Final.

After 90 minutes played and then extra time, the game went to penalties.

Gavin Skelton stepped up to take the final penalty for Gretna but missed.

Hearts won the Scottish Cup but for Gretna, and the 12,000 Gretna fans at Hampden Park, they 'Lived the Dream'.

The dream couldn't last for ever and Gretna Football Club were liquidated by the administrators with debts of four million pounds.

In 2008, a new team was formed at Raydale Park under the leadership of Stuart Rome. The team now play in the Scottish leagues.

In the future, **Gretna Football Club** hopefully may again be, **'Living the Dream'**

Haaf Netters catching fish down the Solway.

Three haaf netters from many years ago.

SOME EXTRA PICTURES FROM DAYS GONE BY.

Old Yard near Gretna Green Railway Station.

Rosebank Café, Corner of Victory Avenue & Glasgow Road.

Lovers Leap Motel at Headless Cross, where Smiths Hotel is now.

The motel rooms behind the main building, picture from the 1960's.

First House in Scotland, The Gretna Chase Hotel and the Callander Hamilton Bridge

First petrol station in Scotland, the Crossways Garage which was owned by William 'Billy' Armstrong for many years

A young team in Gretna in 1947.
Billy Ohara, Ernie Conchie, Tim McCarthy, Tom Graham, Raymond Carruthers, Billy
Moorhead, David Beattie, Joe Martin, Tom Tweddle, Les Muir, Pim Marshall.

Another team in Gretna: Sark Rovers Football Club
Back Row: Bob Cairns (snowball), Sandy Muir, Duncan Neil, Pim Marshall, Harry Barrett,
Ronnie Chandler.
Front Row: Tom Graham, David Milne, George Mitchell, Joe Martin, George Graham.

Brian Davidson

Brian had a successful nationwide business supplying plastic underground drainage systems. He turned his offices in to The Garden House Hotel, now Greens at Gretna Hotel.

Jimmy Norman Jimmy and his sons, Kevin, Craig and Trevor.

A successful grounds maintenance and landscaping business throughout southern Scotland and northern England. They created Halcrow Stadium for greyhound racing. The first race meeting was June 1986. The stadium had a bar and function room for parties, weddings and traditional music events.

George Birnie

George and his lovely wife Ethel ran Birnies Shop in Central Avenue for many years. He created Gretna Golf Club in 1990. The nine hole course and driving range was laid out over 48 acres of former agricultural land. There was a first floor dining room clubhouse with fantastic views over the Solway Firth and Scottish and Cumbrian hills which was also used for parties and functions.

Tibby Marshall

Tibby was a lovely lady who ran the very popular local youth club for many years. She was loved by all the kids in the area. She won the Pensioners Pride Award in 2016.

Family in 1917 outside one of the wooden huts.

Four generations of the Hampson's. My Mam Helen, Dad John, Son Ben, Granddaughter Isla Vienna.

I was born in Sheffield in 1966, had fourteen years there with every school summer holiday in Gretna visiting my grandparents and many relations.

I moved to Gretna in 1980, started as a paperboy then milk boy with Billy Kerr, had lots of jobs but found my passion when the internet came around in 1998, I started helping couples plan their wedding day!

You will have to read my other book called Aisle Be A Success for more on my wonderful life.

Gretna and the surrounding area, what a fantastic place to live, visit and tour.

Hope you enjoyed this book.

Best wishes to you, your family and future generations....

Heath x